STRETCHY
LESSON PLANS

December

Pat Miller

UpstartBooks

Fort Atkinson, Wisconsin

Dedicated to Heather Jankowski, Hancock Elementary, and Laura Householder, André Elementary (Cypress-Fairbanks ISD, Texas)— thanks for suggesting Dewey Bookbody posters.

Credits:
Page 40: "Silent Snowflake" first appeared in *LibrarySparks* magazine, December 2005.

Published by UpstartBooks
W5527 State Road 106
P.O. Box 800
Fort Atkinson, Wisconsin 53538-0800
1-800-448-4887

Contents

Appendix

Bibliography

Introduction

I was inspired to write this book by a woman at a library conference. After one of my presentations, we visited and she said, "I wish I could be a fly on the wall of your library—a fly with a notebook!" This series is for her, and for others who wonder what I do with my students "in the real world." It's also a good way for me to meet my annual resolution to get my lessons more organized!

If you're like me, you want to know how similar my situation is to yours. I'm a library media specialist in a suburban school of 940 students with a full-time aide. Our population is becoming more diverse, and we are adding more ELL classes from PreK through fifth grade. This is my nineteenth year as a librarian, preceded by 15 years as a classroom teacher. I've been a librarian at four schools in diverse situations.

I've been the only librarian for more than 1,200 elementary students (ten classes in most grades), and at a smaller school where many of my students' families were on welfare. I've been "in the rotation" when I taught classes to give the teachers their planning time. I've worked for avid library supporters and one who just wanted me to keep the kids quiet and the parents out of his office. I've worked without an aide, with an aide, and with a cadre of talented mother volunteers.

My current schedule is to see every child every week for check out, but to teach a fixed lesson to intermediates one week, and to their primary partners the next. In a typical month, that means only two lessons per grade. This is a Stretchy Lesson Plan book because I've included more lessons than one would use in a month. The lessons can stretch to fit a number of grade levels and will last for years without repeating if you have my kind of schedule. And best of all, the lessons are bound to trigger some great ideas of your own.

Do I Need These If I Have the Stretchy Library Lessons Books?

The SLL books are invaluable books of lessons for library skills, reading and reference activities, and multicultural and seasonal celebrations. One never has too many lessons from which to choose the best fit for his or her students. One difference is that this series is designed to give you not just lessons, but useful tips, forms, strategies, and reminders that I have developed or discovered over the years. This book is also an organizational tool, correlating additional ideas from the six books of the Stretchy Library Lessons series, the six Collaborative Bridges books, and the first 36 issues of *LibrarySparks*. Add these to your favorite lessons, adapting them to your own students.

Because the lessons from my other books are ones that I often use, those will be referenced in each book. You will have a list of six to eight additional lessons each month from my other books, as well as articles from the first four years of *LibrarySparks* magazine. I write these books not only for you, but also for myself, and I needed a resource that had all those things in one place for easy reference.

In this series, in one place, you have additional lessons for each month, along with useful tips, calendar correlations, forms, patterns, lots of books, and inspiration for your own planning. Whether you wonder how to find a lesson plan form that fits your schedule, how to run a successful book fair, or how to find good literature each week, the answers are here. This is not the definitive plan book, but it will guide you through the year, your library curriculum, and the special events that make your program more fun for students.

How to Use This Book

If you teach in the library, this book is for you. It will help you if you are a certified librarian with a master's degree and extensive experience or if you are a novice librarian in your first elementary library. I hope it will be especially helpful if you are an uncertified aide or generous volunteer. My hat is off to all of you who are constantly looking for ways to meet the needs of your students.

Lessons featured in this book represent many of the lessons I actually have used through the years. Sometimes teachable moments, special events, or collaborative units will bump lessons off your schedule, but these will give you a good start. Each book will include four lessons for grades K–2 and four for grades 3–5. I've also included a number of tips about how I do things in my library that seem to make life easier for my students and me, and might work for you as well.

Each lesson includes:

- **Objective(s):** Why teach this lesson? What student need will it address? How does it correlate to the curriculum?

- **Grades:** This indicates whether the lesson is intended for primary grades or intermediate grades. However, I'm confident that if you are using this book, you are also the person who can adapt any lesson and thrive in any situation.

- **Materials:** These are readily available or easily made and should be gathered before you teach the lesson.

- **Prepare in Advance:** If you teach all grades each day as I do, your lesson materials need to be well organized because there is little time between classes. This section tells you what needs to be made, purchased, or found before your class comes in.

- **Activity Directions:** My schedule is fixed at 45-minute classes, with a few bands of flexible time that can be scheduled by any teacher. The following lessons are designed for approximately 30 minutes and include all forms, worksheets, and patterns that you will need.

- **Resources:** This section lists books to use in place of the featured book or as companion books to it. Use them in a display, share them with teachers or plan extension lessons with them. Web sites are included here and can often be the basis for additional lessons. As I write, the books are in print and the Web sites are current. If you get an error message when using the address, perform a keyword search on the site title. If a book is out of print, check www.amazon.com.

What's Happening This Month?

December is the short school month when your schedule is jostled by an assortment of programs, practices, parties, and other seasonal special events. Enjoy the excitement that children feel especially this time of year.

Set up a birthday display with "Thanks, ___(author name)___, for the presents!" Display a fake birthday cake and attach birthday streamers, party hats, etc. If you don't have a handy bulletin board, use a science fair display board. Attach author pictures if you have them from Web sites, publisher flyers, or book jackets. Then add the birthday books and encourage check out.

Look for 12 pages of birthday celebration ideas in *Stretchy Library Lessons: Seasons and Celebrations*. In your birthday display this month, you can feature books by the following authors:

Author Birthdays			
Jan Brett	Dec. 1	Keiko Kasza	Dec. 23
David Macaulay	Dec. 2	John Langstaff	Dec. 24
Walt Disney	Dec. 5	Eth Clifford	Dec. 25
Mary Downing Hahn	Dec. 9	Pam Muñoz Ryan	Dec. 25
Cornelia Funke	Dec. 10	Jean Van Leeuwen	Dec. 26
William Joyce	Dec. 11	Ted Rand	Dec. 27
Quentin Blake	Dec. 16	Diane Stanley	Dec. 27
Bill Brittain	Dec. 16	Cynthia DeFelice	Dec. 28
Marilyn Sachs	Dec. 18	Molly Bang	Dec. 29
Eve Bunting	Dec. 19	Mercer Mayer	Dec. 30
Jerry Pinkney	Dec. 22	Margery Cuyler	Dec. 31
Avi	Dec. 23	Cynthia Leitich Smith	Dec. 31

Meet these authors in the pages of *LibrarySparks* magazine:

Leo and Diane Dillon, December 2006

Francisco Jiménez, December 2004

David Macaulay, December 2003

Alexis O'Neill, December 2005

Linda Sue Park, December 2006

Vera B. Williams, December 2005

December

Read a New Book Month

Ask teachers to recommend a new children's book they've read recently. Feature the books for check out. Make bookmarks of teacher favorites to distribute to students to encourage them to read a new book.

Deaf Heritage Week

- *All About Sign Language: Talking with your Hands* by Felicia Lowenstein. Enslow Publishers, 2004.

- *Can You Hear a Rainbow? The Story of a Deaf Boy Named Chris* by Jamee Riggio Heelan. Peachtree Publishers, 2002.

- *Deaf Child Crossing* by Marlee Matlin. Simon & Schuster, 2002.

- *The Deaf Musicians* by Pete Seeger and Paul DuBois Jacobs. Putnam, 2006.

- *I Have a Sister—My Sister is Deaf* by Jeanne Peterson. Harper & Row, 1977.

- *I'm Deaf, and It's Okay* by Lorraine Aseltine, Evelyn Mueller, and Nancy Tait. Albert Whitman, 1986.

- *Max Learns Sign Language* by Adria F. Klein. Picture Window Books, 2006.

- *Moses Goes to a Concert* by Isaac Millman. Farrar, Straus and Giroux, 1998.

- *Moses Goes to School* by Isaac Millman. Farrar, Straus and Giroux, 2000.

- *Moses Goes to the Circus* by Isaac Millman. Farrar, Straus and Giroux, 2003.

- *Moses Sees a Play* by Isaac Millman. Farrar, Straus and Giroux, 2004.

- *My Friend Is Deaf* by Anna Levene. Chrysalis Education, 2003.

- *Some Kids Are Deaf* by Lola M. Schaefer. Pebble Books, 2001.

International Language Week (Third week of December)

- *Can You Greet the Whole Wide World? 12 Common Phrases in 12 Different Languages* by Lezlie Evans. Houghton Mifflin, 2006.

- Learning Languages Discovery Library [Seven-book set in Spanish and English]. Rourke Publishing, 2007.

- *People* by Peter Spier. Bantam Doubleday Dell, 1980.

Count to Ten Around the World Activity
Distribute copies of the worksheet on page 9. Assign a number to each student and have them "hop" around the continents on a world map (see page 10) with their fingers as they count.

December Library Events

December School Events

Count to Ten Around the World

	Spelled	Said	Country	Language
1	un	unh	Canada	⅔ English ⅓ French
2	dois	doh-eez	Brazil	Portuguese
3	drei	dry	Germany	German
4	nne	nn-nay	Africa	Swahili
5	٥	kahm-sah	Arab countries	Arabic
6	六	ro-koo	Japan	Japanese
7	일곱	ill-GUP	Korea	Korean
8	οκτω	ohk-toh	Greece	Greek
9	nove	no-vay	Italy	Italian
10	a deich	uh-djeh	Ireland	Gaelic

Silent Snowflake

Objectives: To practice visual perception. To provide a calming activity during hectic pre-holiday weeks.

Grades: K–2

General Materials:

- 25 copies of game board grid

- 20 copies of game board pictures

- 25 sheets of card stock or construction paper (I used red and green.)

- three-ounce paper cups (If you use marshmallows, throw cups away and use new ones for each group.)

- Smarties®, bags of small marshmallows to represent snowballs, or dried beans (If you use Smarties® candy, you won't need cups.)

- 2 glue sticks

- paper cutter

- transparency of game board pictures

- free book coupon if you don't use edible game markers (optional)

- overhead projector and screen

- player and holiday music

Santa Knows

We had a rather large bulletin board that was a monster to decorate. One December we developed the idea of illustrating a scene from "'Twas the Night Before Christmas." Specifically, we decided to illustrate Santa placing his finger beside his nose just before "up the chimney he rose." A precious little kindergartner tugged at my skirt to ask, "Why is Santa picking his nose?" We never did that bulletin board again.

—Anna Allebach, Librarian, Hebron HS, Carrollton, TX

Prepare in Advance:

Use the following steps to make a class set of game boards.

1. Make 25 copies of the holiday symbols grid on page 15. Cut the squares apart in such a way that you have a stack of each symbol laid out in rows on one of your long tables. Cut black border lines off all pictures.

2. Duplicate 25 copies of the blank grid on page 16 and lay them out so you can easily lay a picture on each square. You will need a couple of glue sticks.

3. Pick up a pile of one picture, the candy cane for example. Put a candy cane on the first card in the first square of the first row. Then in the second square of the first row on the second card, third square first row on the third card, etc. Skip every seventh card or so, so it has no candy cane on it. Continue in a methodical manner until all 25 cards have a candy cane or have purposely been skipped. Discard extra pictures.

4. Pick up a second picture, the snowflake for example. Go back to the first card. Skip the first card. Put a snowflake in the third square of the second card, fourth square of the third card, etc. Skip every sixth card or so.

5. If you don't take time to do this methodically, you will end up with a card that has two of the same picture, or two cards that have an identical row or column. Laying the pictures is the most important and most time consuming step of the process, but you the cards will last for many holidays to come.

6. After all of the cards are filled with pictures, carefully use a glue stick to attach each picture to the game board. Make sure the grid lines from the Silent Snowflake card show between the pictures. I use just enough glue to adhere the center of the picture because the lamination will seal the pictures down.

7. Attach completed game sheets to alternating green and red card stock. For best results, let the glue drive overnight.

8. Laminate each game card. Cut the cards apart, leaving a thin margin of lamination around the game board so the laminating film will not separate.

9. Make a transparency of all the symbols on page 15. Cut the squares apart. Put a small black dot on the bottom left corner to prevent showing it reversed and causing confusion when children try to match the picture. Store the transparent pictures in a snack-size zippered plastic bag. Place the snack bag and the cards in a larger plastic zippered bag. Write "Silent Snowflake" on the outside of the bag to facilitate return of materials to it.

10. Buy three-ounce cups and bags of miniature marshmallows (tiny snowballs), or Smarties®. Each child will need either a small cup of marshmallows or a package of candy to use as covers.

Activity Directions:

1. To play, you will need an overhead projector and screen, a game board for each student, a set of transparent pictures, holiday music, a cup of marshmallows, Smarties®, or another small item to use to cover picture squares.

2. It is essential that the game be played in silence. This includes you as the moderator. Once you explain the instructions, do not speak again if at all possible. Instead, play soft holiday music in the background. The fact that you aren't speaking will calm the students. For Classic Cartoon Christmas songs, visit www.toontracker.com/xmasra/xmasra. htm.

3. Explain to the students that Silent Snowflake is played like Bingo. They should each cover the center square that reads "Happy Holidays." Put the matching transparent square on the overhead and project it where all students can see it. Discuss the difference between playing quietly (whispering permitted) and silently (no whispering or other sounds). Only those who play silently can win. Those who play silently will get a special bookmark. Those who don't will disqualify themselves from playing!

4. Tell students that a good strategy to play is to first carefully study the picture. Then they should look across the top row from left to right, then the second row, the third, and so on. They are less likely to miss the picture in this way than if they scan haphazardly around the board.

5. As you place each plastic square, "snap" it onto the stage of the overhead projector. I find that if you bend the card slightly before you pick it up, it will snap when you lay it down or pick it up. This will notify students that you are changing the picture. Play slowly, especially for young students. Give them time to look at the picture and look at every square.

6. Be sure the small black dot on each picture is at the bottom left of the screen. This is to keep the transparent pictures from being flipped over and showing as mirror images of what students actually have on their cards.

7. Students who have five in a row in any direction, including four corners and the center, say "Silent Snowflake." Check their cards to be sure they are correct, then allow them to student eat the marshmallows or candy. Play until you have a specified number of winners or a preset amount of time elapses. Not all will be winners, but I've not had a disappointed player in all the past years because they all get to eat the candy markers when the game is over!

Resources:

Share one of the following titles before or after the Silent Snowflake game:

<u>Fiction</u>

All You Need for a Snowman by Alice Schertle. Harcourt, 2002.

The Best Snowman by Margaret Nash. Picture Window Books, 2003.

The Biggest, Best Snowman by Margery Cuyler. Scholastic, 1998.

The Biggest Snowman Ever by Steven Kroll. Scholastic, 2005.

Black Snowman by Phil Mendez. Scholastic, 1989.

Grandpa's Snowman by Gary Barwin. Annick Press, 2000.

Henry and Mudge and the Snowman Plan: The Nineteenth Book of Their Adventures by Cynthia Rylant. Simon & Schuster, 1999.

Martin MacGregor's Snowman by Lisa Broadie Cook. Walker & Co., 2003.

My Brother Loved Snowflakes: The Story of Wilson A. Bentley, The Snowflake Man by Mary Bahr Fritts. Boyds Mills Press, 2002.

A Really Good Snowman by Daniel J. Mahoney. Clarion Books, 2005.

Snowballs by Lois Ehlert. Harcourt Brace, 1995.

Snowflake Kisses and Gingerbread Smiles by Toni Trent Parker. Scholastic, 2002.

The Snowflake Sisters by J. Patrick Lewis. Atheneum, 2003.

The Snowman by Raymond Briggs. Random House, 1978.

The Snowman's Clothes by Anders Hanson. Abdo Publishing, 2006.

Sophie the Snowflake by Eddie Bowman. Ozark Publishing, 1998.

<u>Nonfiction</u>

Check your shelves, particularly the 551.57 section for books on snow. These are especially good ones to use with young readers:

Flakes and Flurries: A Book About Snow by Josepha Sherman. Picture Window Books, 2004.

I Am Snow by Jean Marzollo. Scholastic, 1998.

Snow is Falling by Franklyn Mansfield Branley. HarperCollins, 2000.

Snowflake Bentley by Jacqueline Briggs Martin. Houghton Mifflin, 1998.

<u>Web Site</u>

Snowman Unit at the Virtual Vine, www.thevirtualvine.com/snowman.html
Includes songs, fingerplays, crafts, and many activities suitable for younger students.

Bookmark Pattern

Have a happy winter holiday from the library!
Use your computer to play in the snow while indoors.

❄ **Cut out paper snowflakes without paper or scissors at:**
snowflakes.lookandfeel.com

❄ **Dress a snowman without getting your hands cold at:**
www.billybear4kids.com/holidays/winter/makesnow/snowman.htm

Silent Snowflake

Happy Holidays!

Write Thank-you Letters

Objectives: To practice letter writing format for an authentic audience. To share books about letter writing.

Grades: K–5

Materials:

- books from suggested list

- copies of thank you stationery on pages 20–22 for each student (note different types for different ages)

- small gift for each student *(optional)*

Get a Job

Our school has a postal system operated by the older students. One morning, my day was brightened by the unintentional irony of a very brief letter from a kindergarten student. "Dear Mrs. Miller, You are a good book reder. You shud get a job as a book reder."

Prepare in Advance:

1. Choose appropriate books from your collection to display or share.

2. Duplicate age appropriate stationery for each class.

3. Order a small gift for each student (try www.orientaltrading.com for Oriental Trading Company), secure freebies from school partners or local businesses, or print coupons in conjunction with teachers and staff. Coupons could be good for a free ice cream in the cafeteria (to be paid for by library funds), a free homework pass, picnic in the library, pass to come to the library with a friend during recess, etc.

Activity Directions:

1. Use books from your collection or the resource list to talk about the various reasons people write letters (to exchange news, keep a diary, thank, congratulate, or commiserate with someone).

2. With the holidays coming up, students may be receiving gifts they love and gifts they don't. Ask, "How many have gotten underwear for a present? Is that a thumbs up kind of present, or thumbs down?" Ask students to talk with the person beside them about a gift they got that they did not like.

3. Read aloud *Thank You, Aunt Tallulah!* to begin this letter writing activity on a funny note. It's 101 degrees at Camp Oggie-Waaa-Waaa and Bettina is happy to get a package. However, it is from her Aunt Tallulah who lives in the Antarctic and sends her hand-knit sweaters, six-fingered gloves, etc. Bettina puts the gifts to unusual uses and sends her aunt and uncle bathing suits made from pinecones, one of which saves her uncle's life. The story gently points out how a gift can be unwanted, but still be given with much love and be deserving of appreciation.

4. Use the stationery on pages 20–22 (picture block for K–1, lined for 2–3, unlined for 4–5) to have students write a thank you to one of the characters in a book you share with

them. Or they can write to thank you for the inexpensive gift or coupon you give each of them. Or they can thank someone in their life that gave them a gift recently, or thank a teacher for something he/she taught them.

5. Students should follow the suggested pattern below (as appropriate to their age) or develop their own.

   a. After the date and greeting, thank the person for the gift. Describe it specifically. Not, "Thanks for the hat," but, "Thank you for the blue and black knit cap." The older the child, the more specific the description.

   b. In the second sentence, tell one thing the gift can be used for. "I will wear it when I go skating with my friends."

   c. Third sentence, say something nice about the giver. "You always make me feel special by remembering me at Christmas/Hanukkah/for my birthday, etc.

   d. Sign with an appropriate close: "Love, your grandson Marty"

6. If there is time, students may want to share their letters with one another.

Resources:

Letters (Picture Book Format)

Bunny Mail by Rosemary Wells. Penguin, 2004.

Dear Baby: Letters from Your Big Brother by Sarah Sullivan. Candlewick Press, 2005.

Dear Mrs. Larue: Letters from Obedience School by Mark Teague. Scholastic, 2002.

Dear Santa: The Letters of James B. Dobbins by Bill Harley. HarperCollins, 2005.

Detective LaRue: Letters from the Investigation by Mark Teague. Scholastic, 2004.

First Year Letters by Julie Danneberg. Charlesbridge, 2003.

The Jolly Postman or Other People's Letters by Janet and Allan Ahlberg. Little, Brown and Company, 1986.

Letters from a Desperate Dog by Eileen Christelow. Clarion Books, 2006.

Love, Lizzie: Letters to a Military Mom by Lisa Tucker McElroy. Albert Whitman, 2005.

The Jolly Christmas Postman by Janet and Allan Ahlberg. Little, Brown and Company, 1991.

Letters (Chapter Book Format)

Dear Levi: Letters from the Overland Trail by Elvira Woodruff. Knopf, 1994.

Letters from Rapunzel by Sara Holmes. HarperCollins, 2007.

Letters from Rifka by Karen Hesse. Puffin, 1992.

Peggy's Letters by Jacqueline Halsey. Orca Books, 2005.

Nonfiction

Letters from Ritang: A Family in Kiribati by Helene Tremblay. Portage & Main Press, 1997.

West from Home: Letters of Laura Ingalls Wilder, San Francisco, 1915 by Laura Ingalls Wilder. HarperCollins, 1974.

Thankfulness

A Father's Day Thank You by Janet Nolan. Albert Whitman, 2007.

Thank You, Aunt Tallulah! by Carmela LaVigna Coyle. Rising Moon, 2006.

Thank You by Kelly Doudna. Abdo Publishing, 2001.

Thank You, Amelia Bedelia by Peggy Parish. HarperCollins, 1993.

Thank You, Mr. Falker by Patricia Polacco. Philomel Books, 1998.

Thank you, Sarah: The Woman Who Saved Thanksgiving by Laurie Halse Anderson. Simon & Schuster, 2002.

Alternative Seating

I have been the librarian at four school libraries and at each I used a different seating solution for when I wanted students to sit on the floor.

At the first school, we had flat pillows with removable/washable covers on them. They were laid out like stadium seating. Carpet squares can be used the same way.

In my second school, my mother and I donated our couches to what we called "The Living Room." Fortunately, they matched and were made from Herculon (remember that scratchy "miracle fiber"?) and so were easy to clean.

I used a large Discover America state map carpet from Highsmith (www.highsmith.com) at the third school. We used it often to locate the setting for books we were sharing, to step in when I named the state, etc. Students would choose a state to sit in or near. DEMCO (www.demco.com) has a carpet with large boxes for each letter of the alphabet. Great to have a child sit in each box. To leave the carpet, they can name a word, a character, a book that begins with that letter.

At my current school library, we sit on padded flooring and upholstered bench seating from Big Cozy Books (www.bigcozybooks.com). The benches are made to look like books standing on their pages with titles on the bench "spines." Other book styles as well as giant pencils, erasers and piles of giant books are available. We've found them to be extremely durable and easy to clean.

To: _____

Thank you for the _____

_____

_____

I will think of you when I use your gift.

Sincerely, _____

Author Visit

Correct student misconceptions and help them build relationships with authors by having them visit your school. Many local authors are quite affordable and will do an excellent presentation. The following information is also relevant for illustrators.

How to Find an Author

- To find an author from your area, contact the regional chapter of the Society of Children's Book Writers and Illustrators, www.scbwi.org/regions.htm. Each chapter's page often includes a link to a speaker's bureau so you can contact the author or illustrator directly. Local authors are often financially more affordable because they have lower expenses. Presenters should be able to provide references for you.

- You can also contact authors directly through their Web sites. You can search the Index to Internet Sites: Children's and Young Adults' Authors & Illustrators (falcon.jmu.edu/~ramseyil/biochildhome.htm) but the links are not always reliable. The Children's Book Council provides links to authors and illustrators who are published by members of the CBC and whose Web pages showcase these books. Find contact information at www.cbcbooks.org/contacts/visits.html or subscribe to www.TeachingBooks.net (free trial avialable).

How to Pay for an Author

- Finance your author with activity funds, book fair profits, fine/damage money, or PTA/PTO grants. Title 1 and ESL funds can often be used to hire authors. If it is feasible at your campus, sell pencils. At one of my schools, I made more money on pencils than on my book fairs! We sold pencils for 10 minutes each morning, just before the first bell.

How to Prepare for an Author

- For best results, students should be familiar with the author and his/her books before he/she arrives. Order copies of the author's books in advance so many of them can be read to the students. If you don't have time to read enough books to the students, ask teachers to help. For every book they read to students, they can get their name in a drawing for an autographed book. Or you might allow teachers to acquire their own copies in advance so they can read them to their students (and get them autographed the day of the visit). "Visit" the author in advance by sharing his/her biography and picture with students. You can get this information by:

- writing to the author in care of his/her publisher

- visiting the author's Web site

- reading from the jacket copy

- visiting Teaching Books, www.teachingbooks.net and watching/reading interviews from the Author Programs section

- visiting Learning About the Author and Illustrator, www.scils.rutgers.edu/~kvander/AuthorSite/index.html

How to Get Books

- Check with the author. Especially if the author is local, he/she may want to provide the books because they earn more money if they do. If they decline to bring books, contact your local independent bookseller. Your business is appreciated, and they will give you personal service.

- If you don't have one, make arrangements with the closest chain bookstore. You can often get a discount from either of these providers which you can pass on to students or charge full price and use the difference to help defray the cost of the author. Ask if you can return unsold copies. Usually you will get a bigger discount if you order exactly what you sell. The advantage to ordering extra and returning unsold copies is that you can take orders up to the day before the author arrives.

Countdown to an Author Visit

Four Months in Advance: (Some very well-known authors require a year or more in advance)

- Ascertain availability of the author by writing to him/her at their Web site. (No Web site for your author? Get contact information from his/her publisher.) What does (s)he charge for a visit? How many talks per school? Will (s)he speak to two schools in one day? Does (s)he charge for expenses? Will (s)he need a rental car or can we drive him/her? Will (s)he book his/her own airline ticket?

- Find out which schools are interested in sharing the author. After the other schools sign up, arrange a schedule for the visit, and send copies to each librarian and to the author. Then, paired schools can arrange their schedule and inform the chair of the schedule and the lunch location. Often, authors offer a discount to the school that arranges multiple visits.

- Make hotel and rental car arrangements if the author is not local. If the author doesn't want a car, who will pick him/her up from the airport and make the return trip? Does the author prefer a non-smoking room? Does he/she need a ground floor room? This is often helpful if the author will be autographing a lot of books and may have to cart them to and from the hotel room.

Three Months in Advance:

- Contact the book vendor to find out the logistics of ordering. Local authors often prefer to bring and sell their own books. This gives them a larger profit on their own sales—a perk they appreciate. A perk for you is that checks can be made directly to them and no paperwork is needed.

- Generate an order form. I like to include copies of the book covers, a brief description of the book, and ordering information. See page 27 for an example.

- Decide how the author will be paid and make arrangements for his/her check. Generate a contract (see example on page 28) that can also be used as the receipt. Authors truly appreciate receiving their check when they visit, so arrange to pay your author on the day of the performance if this is workable in your financial system.

Two Months in Advance:

- Begin reading the author's books to students, making them available to teachers as well. Share the author's biography, picture, and Web site. Make sure the visit is on the school calendar, reserve the space in which the author will speak, and plan your publicity.

- Prepare a schedule for the author to speak. Keep the author's size limits in mind. When making a schedule, allow bathroom breaks between groups and enough time for autographing.

- Order books. Estimate quantities based on student interest in the past, or on the success of previous book fairs. This can be arranged with your vendor. Some require more notice than others, often depending on the author.

One Month in Advance (or in the time frame arranged with vendor):

- Send out order forms. Request checks be made to either the school or the author. Find out if it is necessary to collect tax. Whether you have checks made to your school or the vendor, be sure the vendor or author will pay the tax for the school. One reason to have the checks made to the school would be in the case of using the book sale as a fundraiser.

- Confirm hotel and car arrangements. Check with author to confirm flight information if needed. Does he/she have any food preferences or special needs?

One Week in Advance:

- Prepare books for autographing. To prevent errors and make it easier for your authors, place a sticky note on the title page with the name of the person requesting the autograph. Place the order slip in the back of the book to make distribution easier. Be sure the student name in the margin is showing at the top of the slip. If students order multiple books, duplicate the order form so a slip can be placed in the back of each book to prevent confusion.

- Make a banner or sign to welcome the author to your school. Can a group of students (Student Council?) be on hand to welcome the author along with you, and escort him/her to the library? Maybe a welcome message can be put up on your marquee.

Day of the Visit:

- Have coffee, tea, and/or soft drinks available as well as cold water. Light breakfast pastries will be hospitable if you have an author in the morning. Snacks and chocolate are usually appreciated. You might want to have a welcome bag prepared for the author containing small items representing your school as well as snack items. Be considerate of those on planes since they will have to carry your gift back in their luggage. Gifts I have most appreciated in my travels were those that somehow represented the area in which I spoke.

- Be on time to pick up your author as prearranged, or be ready to welcome him or her when he/she arrives. Make sure you have informed the author of where to park. Help bring in props, books, and other materials the author may have.

- Have table(s), microphone, and other equipment set up in the speaking area. Have books on display. Authors often bring their own, but those who fly may have to leave them behind.

- Seat children promptly, with younger ones in the front for best viewing.

- With author permission, take photos of the author speaking, and posed with you and with students. Make a scrapbook of author visits, including the author's autograph—students enjoy looking at the photos of the "real" authors who have been to your school. If possible, have a place in the library where the author can sign the wall or a bulletin board for a permanent record of all the writers and illustrators that have visited your library. Submit the photos to your yearbook coordinator.

- Be prompt in meeting your school partner for lunch, and allow enough time for the author to relax and eat. It takes a lot of energy to be "on" for a number of visits in the day, and lunch is a nice break.

- You may want to plan a dinner for the author and librarians if the author is doing an extended visit. Most evenings, the author will appreciate down time to re-energize. Many use the time away from home to write. Provide maps of local malls, theaters, points of interest, and restaurants for those on an extended stay.

- Distribute autographed books to students as promptly as possible.

After the Visit:

- Thank the author for visiting. Enclose some thank-you notes from students. Ask students to include one thing they learned and one question they have. Student letters are cherished by authors. Avoid having students copy a form letter. This is uninspiring for them and impersonal for the author who receives them. If students are unable to write, have them draw a picture and write thank you with their name. Be sure students know they are unlikely to receive a personal letter. If teachers send their letters clipped together, authors can send a class letter.

- Authors and illustrators appreciate photos of themselves in action and with students. Be sure to secure parent permission before sending photos to the author. The author may wish to include the photo on his/her Web site, so secure permission to send the photos as .gif files via e-mail.

GET YOUR GROUNDHOG BOOK BEFORE THEY DiSAPPEAR!

Author Pat Miller will be visiting our school on January 21. Mrs. Miller is a school librarian in Texas and has been writing for nearly 10 years.

She will talk to grades K–2 about how a book is made, and to grades 3–5 about how she gets her ideas and the writing process.

Mrs. Miller will be autographing books during her visit. She would love to sign one for your child.

Substitute Groundhog
(Albert Whitman, 2006)

When Dr. Owl prescribes two days of bed rest for his flu, Groundhog knows he will have to get a substitute to do his Groundhog Day duty. But during tryouts, each animal has a problem until a very unlikely candidate proves to be the perfect substitute.

Junior Library Guild Selection, 2007

Price per book—$15.95

- -

Autograph to: _____

Deliver to: _____

Price per book is $15.95. Make checks payable to our school.

Deadline for orders is January 18.

(For additional copies, write information on the back of this form.)

Teacher's Name:

Sample Author Visit Contract

Author Visit Contract

Author Name: _____

Author Mailing Address: _____

_____

_____

SSN: _____ – _____ – _____

E-mail address: _____

Date and times of presentations: _____

Fee agreement: _____

Expenses: _____

Equipment needed: _____

May we take your picture for school use? _____

Contact person: _____

School address: _____

_____

_____

School Phone number: _____

School E-mail address: _____

Please sign and return both copies in the enclosed SASE.
One copy will be returned to you with your check.

Poinsettia Bract Facts

Objectives: To locate five facts about a person they enjoyed reading about. To know a biography is the story of someone's life.

Grades: 3–5

Materials:

- transparencies

- overhead pens

- simple biographies about famous people when they were children

- books about poinsettias (see bibliography)

- pads of sticky notes and pencils for student pairs

Books for the Holiday

Early this month, decide whether you will let students take books home over the holidays. We do send books home since this is often prime reading time. We ask students not to take their books on their trips with them, but to only read them at home. As a result, we have only lost a few, but many were read in the weeks without school.

Prepare in Advance:

1. Make a transparency of the brief biography on page 32.

2. Make a transparency of the poinsettia bracts on pages 33–34. Cut the bracts apart. Cut out the small flower for the center.

3. Set up the overhead projector and screen where all can see.

Activity Directions:

1. Ask students to predict who Joel Poinsett was. List their predictions on a blank transparency without comment. Then ask them to listen and read along to see what new information they learn.

2. Place the transparency of Poinsett's story on the overhead so students can follow along as you read. After reading, check their list of predictions to see if any were correct. Ask students to tell you some facts they remember. As they say them, underline them on the transparency.

3. Show students how to write the events on the bracts of the poinsettia. When you have six facts, put the flower center of the poinsettia in the middle of the screen, and arrange the fact bracts around it to form a poinsettia. Be sure one bract has the name of the person written large and clear. This should be at the clock position of three on the poinsettia.

4. Students can prepare and display brief interesting facts about interesting people based on simple biographies. My students have enjoyed working with biographies that describe the lives of famous people when they were children. They seem more human and students relate to them better.

5. Pair students and let them work with biographies selected from your collection, particularly ones featured in the biography that follows. Have them use small sticky notes to attach to pages where they locate a Wow! or new fact. When they have found five or six interesting facts, they can rewrite them in their own words on the bracts. Once the bracts are finished, students cut them out and glue them on a sheet of red construction paper, being sure that the name is in 3:00 position on each one and the small flower is in the center. Display the poinsettia books and the biographies with the completed poinsettia fact bract biographies.

Resources:

Poinsettias

Decking the Halls: Folklore and Traditions of Christmas Plants by Linda Allen. Willow Creek Press, 2000.

The Gift of the Poinsettia = El regalo de la flor de nochebuena by Pat Mora & Charles Ramírez Berg. Piñata Books, 1995.

The Legend of the Poinsettia retold and illustrated by Tomie dePaola. Putnam, 1994.

The Miracle of the First Poinsettia: A Mexican Christmas Story by Joanne Oppenheim. Barefoot Books, 2006.

Suggested Childhood Biographies

Abe Lincoln: The Boy Who Loved Books by Kay Winters. Simon & Schuster, 2003.

American Boy: The Adventures of Mark Twain by Don Brown. Houghton Mifflin, 2003.

Anne Frank by Jonatha A. Brown. Weekly Reader Early Learning Library, 2004.

The Boy on Fairfield Street: How Ted Geisel Grew Up to Become Dr. Seuss by Kathleen Krull. Random House, 2004.

Childhoods of Famous Americans biography series from Aladdin Paperbacks.

Dakota Fanning by Joanne Mattern. Mitchell Lane Publishers, 2006.

Eleanor by Barbara Cooney. Viking, 1996.

George Rogers Clark: Boy of the Northwest Frontier by Katharine E. Wilkie. Patria Press, 2004.

Jump! From the Life of Michael Jordan by Floyd Cooper. Philomel Books, 2004.

Make Your Mark, Franklin Roosevelt! by Judith St. George. Philomel Books, 2007.

My Brother Martin: A Sister Remembers Growing Up With the Rev. Dr. Martin Luther King Jr. by Christine King Farris. Simon & Schuster, 2003.

Odd Boy Out: Young Albert Einstein by Don Brown. Houghton Mifflin, 2004.

Rare Treasure: Mary Anning and Her Remarkable Discoveries by Don Brown. Houghton Mifflin, 1999.

Take the Lead, George Washington! by Judith St. George. Philomel Books, 2005.

Tomas Rivera by Jane Medina. Harcourt, 2004.

Uncommon Traveler: Mary Kingsley in Africa by Don Brown. Houghton Mifflin, 2000.

When Abraham Talked to the Trees by Elizabeth Van Steenwyk. Eerdmans, 2000.

Young Thomas Edison by Michael Dooling. Holiday House, 2004.

You're on Your Way, Teddy Roosevelt! by Judith St. George. Philomel Books, 2004.

Joel Roberts Poinsett

Joel Roberts Poinsett was the first American ambassador to Mexico. He was visiting Mexico in 1828 when he saw a beautiful plant with large red and green leaves. He took cuttings home to South Carolina.

The plant, called Euphorbia pulcherrima, did well and became popular. The flower was beloved, the name was not. William Prescott, a horticulturist, named the plant poinsettia in honor of the man who first brought it to the United States.

Poinsettias are often seen during the winter holidays. Today it has been bred to be white, pink, mottled, and striped as well as deep red. The actual flowers are tiny and yellow and are surrounded by red petal-like leaves called "bracts."

Poinsettia Bract Patterns

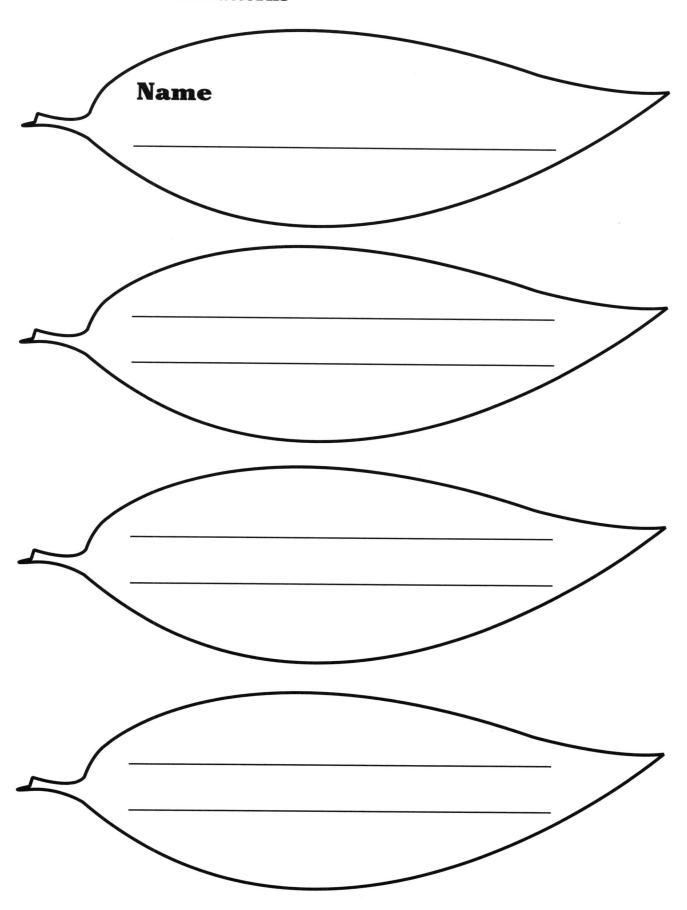

Name

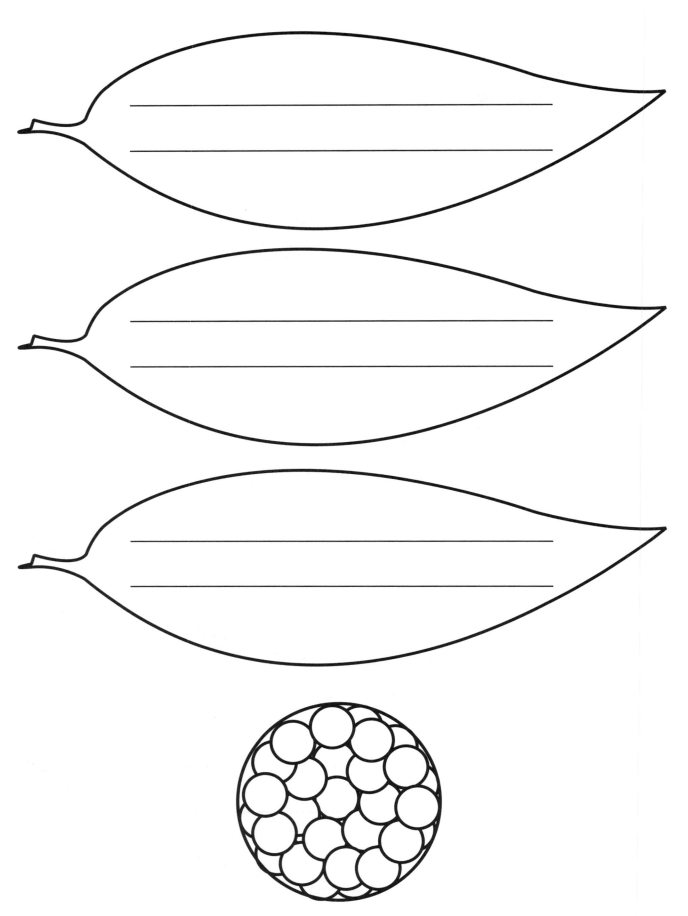

Evergreen Memories

Objectives: To share holiday memories of different customs. To learn more about evergreen trees.

Grades: K–5

Materials:

- collection of books from list on page 36

- copies of page 37 for each student

- pencil

- notebook, binding machine, or other way to make student contributions into books for the library

Prepare in Advance:

1. Duplicate copies of the activity sheet.

2. Sharpen pencils.

3. Set up display of books.

4. Locate pictures of evergreen trees. Use a book from your collection, or show pictures from www.dnr.state.wi.us/org/caer/ce/eek/veg/trees/evergreen.htm.

Activity Directions:

1. Begin by sharing the following talking points:

   a. Evergreen trees are found in every state of the Union. They are often coniferous (seeds are hidden in cones), and have round or flat needle-shaped leaves. They are never totally without their leaves, shedding them instead as they grow. Evergreens include varieties of cedar, fir, hemlock, pine, and spruce. Show students pictures of evergreens from your books or the Web site listed above. Discuss their experience with them.

Boss of the Books

The first graders were seated on the floor in a line, waiting to leave the library. I was walking down the line so they could show me which books they had chosen. When I got to the girl at the end, she had a question for me. "Aren't you the principal?" I assured her I wasn't. "Well, I think you are. You are the principal of the library," she replied.

b. Other things are referred to as being "evergreen." Subjects for books that are evergreen are ones that people always want to read about—like dog stories. For some the beach is an evergreen vacation spot because they will go there every chance they get. Evergreen memories are those we will remember all our lives.

c. In December and January, there are many celebrations that involve family traditions and so create evergreen memories.

2. For this activity, students can share a holiday memory that is so special they think it will be evergreen—remembered long after many other memories are forgotten. Give them an example from your own holiday tradition. Also give them an example that is not from a holiday. For grades K–2, simply sharing the memories will be enough. Encourage them to think of sensory details before sharing.

4. In grades 3–5, have students use a blank sheet of paper to brainstorm unforgettable memories. Prompts might include the names of relatives, places, foods, activities, favorite traditions, etc. Once their memory has been selected, ask them to list sensory details about that memory. For example, if cutting down a tree to decorate in their home is a memory, how did that sound, smell, feel, and look? Were there any tastes? (Maybe the hot chocolate they drink after coming in from the cold.)

5. Based on their sensory details, have students write about an Evergreen Memory they have. You may want to bind their work into books. If so, ask their permission to do so. They may want to take their original home and have a copy put in the book. Children may want to decorate the memory page and return it at a later date.

Resources:

Bristlecone Pines by Kelli M. Brucken. KidHaven Press, 2005.

Christmas Tree Farming by Ann Purmell. Holiday House, 2006.

Decking the Halls: Folklore and Traditions of Christmas Plants by Linda Allen. Willow Creek Press, 2000.

Evergreen Trees by John F. Prevost. Abdo & Daughters, 1996.

Evergreens are Green by Susan Canizares. Scholastic, 1998.

The Life Cycle of a Pine Tree by Linda Tagliaferro. Capstone Press, 2007.

Pine Tree by Jason Cooper. Rourke Publishing, 2004.

Evergreen Memories

by _____

_____

_____

_____

_____

_____

_____

_____

_____

_____

_____

Grandparents Day

In 1978, President Jimmy Carter proclaimed that National Grandparents Day would be celebrated annually on the first Sunday after Labor Day. Declare a second Grandparents Day just before Thanksgiving or Christmas when so many of them are in town to share the holidays with their grandchildren.

I organized the Grandparents Day celebration for seven years at one of my schools. The library hosted the coffee and doughnuts. In the library, we had the book fair set up. A special lunch was served by the cafeteria and each grade level held activities they thought would be fun for students and adults and would show off some of their learning.

Here are some things to think about if you would like to schedule a Grandparents Day.

Publicity

Send home a flyer weeks in advance with an RSVP form (see page 41).

Welcome: Post a welcome sign on the school marquee. Ask early arrivals if a few of them would like to lead the pledge on the morning announcements. All grandmothers receive a paper flower "corsage" made in art by students. All grandparents wear name tags with their name and "Grandmother of Suzy, Ben, and Rachel" printed in advance. Have some blanks for latecomers.

Schedule: Plan the schedule with the teachers. Help them brainstorm activities that will entertain grandparents and still fit their curriculum. Many review activities with games, drill downs, spelling bees, etc., will be enjoyed by children and adults alike. Ask if each class would like a grandparent reader. When? Make a master schedule for readers. Send a copy of the Grandparent Day schedule home in advance so families can plan their day. Have copies on hand to distribute as needed. (See sample on page 40.)

Map: Be sure to print a map on the back of the schedule and add signage in the halls if needed to clarify where classes are located. Make it clear on the map where the adult bathrooms are located.

Food: Use the RSVP forms to order coffee and doughnuts. We used this time as a meet and greet outside the library while students settled into class. Our cafeteria manager was able to juggle our district menu a little so the turkey meal fell on the day we chose for Grandparents Day. Give her the RSVP numbers in advance. We sold tickets. Those who didn't order their ticket(s) in time could bring lunch with them. Order coffee, juice, and pastries for the RSVPs and have parent volunteers or student council members on hand to serve.

Grandparent Book Display: Weeks before the event, display grandparent books and share a number of them with students prior to the big day to promote discussion and publicity. Inevitably, students whose grandparents cannot attend may feel sad. Have a large bulletin board for them to display a photo of them with their grandparents (be sure to return it) so they can feel included. Perhaps those absent grandparents can be encouraged to write a letter, send it to the school in advance (and in secret) and it can be delivered to the students on the big day so they will feel their loved ones are with them in spirit. You can also share the book *Zero Grandparents*.

Adapt the forms on pages 40–41 to fit your needs.

Grandparent Books to Share:

<u>**Primary Grades**</u>

38 Ways to Entertain Your Grandparents by Dette Hunter. Annick Press, 2002.

A Grand Celebration: Grandparents in Poetry selected by Carol G. Hittleman and Daniel R. Hittleman. Wordsong/Boyds Mills Press, 2002.

Grandparents' Day by Nikki Tate. Annick Press, 2004.

Hooray for Grandparents' Day! by Nancy Carlson. Viking, 2000.

Meet my Grandparents by J. Jean Robertson. Rourke Publishing, 2007.

My Grandparents by Mary Auld. Gareth Stevens, 2004.

Robert Lives with His Grandparents by Martha Whitmore Hickman. Albert Whitman, 1995.

Zero Grandparents by Michelle Edwards. Harcourt, 2001.

<u>**Intermediate Grades**</u>

Grandparents! by Roser Capdevila. Kane/Miller, 2001.

Grandparent Poems compiled by John Micklos, Jr. Wordsong/Boyds Mill Press, 2004.

Grandma & Grandpa's Big Book of Fun: Great Things to Make and Do with Grandkids by Jean Luttrell. Marlor Press, 2001.

Sample Grandparents Day Schedule

Grandparents Day Schedule School Name, Date		
Time	**Location**	**Event/Activity**
8:30–9:00	Library	Coffee and doughnuts for guests
All day	Library	Shop the book fair with your grandchild(ren)
Hourly	Gym	Join us for square dancing
9:00–9:30	Grade 1	Holiday songs and fingerplays
9:30–10:00	Grade 3	Reader's Theater performances
10:00–10:30	Grade K	Grandparent Bingo
10:30–12:30	Cafeteria	Lunch on the half hour
12:00–1:00	Grade 2	Holiday Poetry
1:00–1:30	Grade 5 in the cafeteria	Readings and musical performances
1:30–2:30	Grade 4	Spelling Bee and Math Drill Down
2:30–3:30	Choir	Choir, Holiday Program

(See map on reverse)

10th Annual Lincoln Elementary School
Grandparents Day!

★ Be our guest for coffee, juice, and doughnuts in the library from 8:30–9:30.

★ Stay for classroom events throughout the school and the day.

★ A special lunch will be served by our cafeteria.
Come dine with your grandchild!

Please send in the completed reservation form by _____.
(If you don't reserve lunch in time, feel free to bring your own.)

Menu

Sliced turkey breast with gravy   Cranberry sauce

Cornbread dressing   Cherry cobbler

Green beans   Iced tea or milk

Mashed potatoes

We will be coming for Grandparents Day on _____.

Name(s) of adults (as wanted on name tags):

_____

_____

Related to: _____ Teacher _____
(name one grandchild to receive your meal tickets)

★ How many adults for coffee and pastries? _____

★ How many adults for lunch? _____

I enclose _____ for my lunch tickets. (Cost is _____ for each adult.)

Point of View

Objectives: To notice the perspective/point of view in illustrations.

Grades: K–2 (Optional activity for grades 3–5.)

Materials:

- *Christmas for a Kitten* or other book (see resource list)

- sheets of paper cut lengthwise, one half for each student (optional)

- pencils *(optional)*

Prepare in Advance:

1. Locate books. Read them in advance to note the perspectives.

2. If you plan to do the optional activity, get drawing paper and sharpen the pencils.

Enough Already!

I was perched in my rocking chair, talking with kindergartners before reading a large, appealing book called *A Splendid Friend Indeed.* I was enjoying the session and the children seemed motivated and involved by the discussion. It became evident that not everyone was enjoying themselves when a little girl suddenly yelled, "Would you just read the book?!"

Activity Directions:

1. Use this activity with any of the suggested books in the resource list or one of your favorites. I use *Christmas for a Kitten* because every page provides a different perspective of the kitten. The story is about a kitten taken from its mother and put into a sack, which is thrown from a truck with a snarl, "Too many cats!" After trying to live alone in the snowy woods, the kitten hitches a ride on a newly cut tree into the trunk of a family's car. At their home, the little cat discovers an unfriendly dog, drinks Santa's milk, chews on the cookies, plays with the ornaments, and climbs the tree. When another stranger with a bag enters the room, the kitten is terrified until a gentle hand pulls him from the tree and takes him home to the North Pole.

2. Tell students that writers tell stories from a character's or person's point of view. Illustrators show the picture from a variety of perspectives, or viewpoints. Sometimes it is as if the reader is looking down at the picture from the sky (bird's-eye view), sometimes from the ground up, etc. After you read each page, ask students to tell from which viewpoint the picture is painted. If you prefer, you can read the entire book, and then go back and look at the illustrations again.

3. Optional for grades 3–5: Use the book to help students draw from perspective. Give students a sheet of paper. Have them fold it in half and number the squares 1–4 (front and back). Tell them they will be drawing the same thing from three points of view. In square one, they should write their name and the title of the picture. Before drawing, they should label each square at the top. Square two will say, "From the side." Square three will say, "Overhead looking down" (bird's-eye view). Square four will say, "Ground looking up" (kitten's-eye view). Ask them to draw a simple item (a cake on a table, a car on the road, a person) in each square. They can discuss with a partner how their pictures will change before they begin drawing if that helps them.

Resources:

Christmas for a Kitten by Robin Pulver. Albert Whitman, 2003.

Hey, Little Ant by Phillip Hoose and Hannah Hoose. Ten Speed Press, 1998.

Mouse Views: What the Class Pet Saw by Bruce McMillan. Holiday House, 1993.

What the Sea Saw by Stephanie St. Pierre. Peachtree Publishers, 2006.

What's Up, What's Down? by Lola M. Schaefer. Greenwillow Books, 2002.

Additional Lessons for December

Stretchy Library Lesson Series

Stretchy Library Lessons: Library Skills
"Caldecott Challenge" (1–3), pp. 14–19. Everything you need to run a Caldecott Challenge to encourage students to read and examine some of the best art in recent picture books.
"Real or Imagined?" (K–2), pp. 26–29. How do you tell the difference between fiction and nonfiction? Can students spot it in comparing two books on the same topic?

Stretchy Library Lessons: More Library Skills
"Kinds of Fiction" (3–5) pp. 51–56. Learn the types of fiction and how they fit into a manipulative graphic organizer to facilitate understanding and eliminate confusion.

Stretchy Library Lessons: Reading Activities
"Nonfiction Grabber" (K–5), pp. 72–78. Three ways to engage readers before reading nonfiction, Take Three, the Frog-O-Matic Answer Machine, and I Have Who Has?

Stretchy Library Lessons: Research Skills
"Using the Index" (3–5), pp. 43–46. Have an information race using an index, the table of contents, and the body of a nonfiction book, and learn the advantages of the index.

Stretchy Library Lessons: Seasons & Celebrations
"Winter" (3–5), pp. 50–54. Tacky the Penguin reader's theater script, seasonal tic tac toe, tracking animals, mystery master logic puzzle, and wide selection of books and Web sites.

Collaborative Bridges Series: Primary

Me, Myself & You
"Family" pp. 27–31. Learn about grandparents, heritage, simple paper quilting, life now and life in grandparents' time, and making personal time lines.

Collaborative Bridges Series: Intermediate
by Aileen Kirkham

Investigations
"December: Christmas, Hanukkah & Kwanzaa" pp. 16–27. Compare and contrast December's holidays with Holiday Baseball, sign language, and international traditions.
"Rocks and Minerals Unite!" pp. 37–45. Play a game, visit a virtual rock gallery, create gemstones, make the recipes: sedimentary dip, igneous dip, and metamorphic poop.

LibrarySparks Correlation

If you are a *LibrarySparks* subscriber like me, you may overlook the great lessons in your back issues as you plan for future lessons. To help us both (part of my resolution to be more organized), each month will include references to additional lessons in *LibrarySparks* magazine. If you are not a subscriber, you still have access to the articles with an * on the *LibrarySparks* Web site: www.librarysparks.com. Every issue online and in the magazine includes a calendar with daily books, events, and suggested activities. Most are quick and easy.

December 2003 (Theme: Flight)
Booktalks: December Celebrations (K–2, 3–5)
Crafts: Winter Holidays (K–2)
Curriculum Connections: First Flight! (K–2, 3–5)
Keep 'Em Reading: Nonfiction Flying (3–5)
Library Lessons: Winging Around the Library (Using the Library) (3–5)
Meet the Author: David Macaulay (K–2, 3–5)
Storytime: Snowman (K–2)

December 2004 (Theme: Winter Holidays)
Storytime: The Weather Outside is Frightful (K–2)
Curriculum Connections: Winter Holidays Across the Curriculum (K–2, 3–5)
Keep 'Em Reading: World Wide Words (K–2, 3–5)
Meet the Author: Francisco Jiménez (3–5)
Library Skills: Organizing Holiday Research (3–5)
Library Skills: Internet Research—The Mystery of the Holiday Heist (3–5)
Literature: Library Lessons for *The Bad Beginning* (3–5)

December 2005 (Theme: Bullies and Peacemakers)
Meet the Author: Alexis O'Neill (K–2)
Reader's Theater: *The Recess Queen* (K–3)
Storytime: Gingerbread Jubilee (K–2)
Curriculum Connections: Bullies and Peacemakers (K–2, 3–5)
Meet the Author: Vera B. Williams (K–2, 3–5) with extensions and activities
Skills: How to Analyze Online Sources (4–5)
Literature: The Chronicles of Narnia (3–5)
Keep 'Em Reading: Sweet Reading (National Chocolate Day) (3–5)
December 2006 (Theme: What's Cooking?)
Curriculum Connections: Ethnic Edibles (K–2, 3–5)
Keep 'Em Reading: Around the World with Mystery Menus (3–5)
Reader's Theater: *Bee-bim Bop!* (1–3)
Storytime: All Around the Kitchen (K–2)

Literature: Ice Cream: The Full Scoop (3–5)
Meet the Illustrators: Leo and Diane Dillon (K–2, 3–5) with extension activities
Library Skills: Who You Gonna Call? (Professional)
Meet the Author: Linda Sue Park (1–3)
Keep 'Em Reading: *Charlotte's Web* Premiere Party (K–2, 3–5)

Bibliography

A

Ahlberg, Janet and Allen. *The Jolly Christmas Postman.* Little, Brown and Company, 1991.

Ahlberg, Janet and Allen. *The Jolly Postman or Other People's Letters.* Little, Brown and Company, 1986.

Allen, Linda. *Decking the Halls: Folklore and Traditions of Christmas Plants.* Willow Creek Press, 2000.

Anderson, Laurie Halse. *Thank you, Sarah: The Woman Who Saved Thanksgiving.* Simon & Schuster, 2002.

Auld, Mary. *My Grandparents.* Gareth Stevens, 2004.

B

Barwin, Gary. *Grandpa's Snowman.* Annick Press, 2000.

Bloom, Suzanne. *A Splendid Friend Indeed.* Boyds Mills Press, 2005.

Bowman, Eddie. *Sophie the Snowflake.* Ozark Publishing, 1998.

Branley, Franklyn Mansfield. *Snow is Falling.* HarperCollins, 2000.

Briggs, Raymond. *The Snowman.* Random House, 1978.

Brown, Don. *American Boy: The Adventures of Mark Twain.* Houghton Mifflin, 2003.

Brown, Don. *Odd Boy Out: Young Albert Einstein.* Houghton Mifflin, 2004.

Brown, Don. *Rare Treasure: Mary Anning and Her Remarkable Discoveries.* Houghton Mifflin, 1999.

Brown, Don. *Uncommon Traveler: Mary Kingsley in Africa.* Houghton Mifflin, 2000.

Brown, Jonatha A. *Anne Frank.* Weekly Reader Early Learning Library, 2004.

Brucken, Kelli M. *Bristlecone Pines.* KidHaven Press, 2005.

C

Canizares, Susan. *Evergreens are Green.* Scholastic, 1998.

Capdevila, Roser. *Grandparents!* Kane/Miller, 2001.

Carlson, Nancy. *Hooray for Grandparents' Day!* Viking, 2000.

Christelow, Eileen. *Letters from a Desperate Dog.* Clarion Books, 2006.

Cook, Lisa Broadie. *Martin MacGregor's Snowman.* Walker & Co., 2003.

Cooney, Barbara. *Eleanor.* Viking, 1996.

Cooper, Floyd. *Jump! From the Life of Michael Jordan.* Philomel Books, 2004.

Cooper, Jason. *Pine Tree.* Rourke Publishing, 2004.

Coyle, Carmela LaVigna. *Thank You, Aunt Tallulah!* Rising Moon, 2006.

Cuyler, Margery. *The Biggest, Best Snowman.* Scholastic, 1998.

D

Danneberg, Julie. *First Year Letters.* Charlesbridge, 2003.

dePaola, Tomie. *The Legend of the Poinsettia.* Putnam, 1994.

Dooling, Michael. *Young Thomas Edison.* Holiday House, 2004.

Doudna, Kelly. *Thank You.* Abdo Publishing Co., 2001.

E

Edwards, Michelle. *Zero Grandparents.* Harcourt, 2001.

Ehlert, Lois. *Snowballs.* Harcourt Brace, 1995.

F

Farris, Christine King. *My Brother Martin: A Sister Remembers Growing Up With the Rev. Dr. Martin Luther King Jr.* Simon & Schuster, 2003.

Fritts, Mary Bahr. *My Brother Loved Snowflakes: The Story of Wilson A. Bentley, The Snowflake Man.* Boyds Mills Press, 2002.

H

Halsey, Jacqueline. *Peggy's Letters.* Orca Books, 2005.

Hanson, Anders. *The Snowman's Clothes.* Abdo Publishing, 2006.

Harley, Bill. *Dear Santa: The Letters of James B. Dobbins.* HarperCollins, 2005.

Hesse, Karen. *Letters from Rifka.* Puffin, 1992.

Hickman, Martha Whitmore. *Robert Lives with His Grandparents.* Albert Whitman, 1995.

Hittleman, Carol G. and Daniel R. *A Grand Celebration: Grandparents in Poetry.* Wordsong/Boyds Mills Press, 2002.

Holmes, Sara. *Letters from Rapunzel.* HarperCollins, 2007.

Hoose, Phillip and Hannah. *Hey, Little Ant.* Ten Speed Press, 1998.

Hunter, Dette. *38 Ways to Entertain Your Grandparents.* Annick Press, 2002.

K

Kroll, Steven. *The Biggest Snowman Ever.* Scholastic, 2005.

Krull, Kathleen. *The Boy on Fairfield Street: How Ted Geisel Grew Up to Become Dr. Seuss.* Random House, 2004.

L

Lewis, J. Patrick. *The Snowflake Sisters*. Atheneum, 2003.

Luttrell, Jean. *Grandma & Grandpa's Big Book of Fun: Great Things to Make and Do with Grandkids*. Marlor Press, 2001.

M

Mahoney, Daniel J. *A Really Good Snowman*. Clarion Books, 2005.

Martin, Jacqueline Briggs. *Snowflake Bentley*. Houghton Mifflin, 1998.

Marzollo, Jean. I Am Snow. Scholastic, 1998.

Mattern, Joanne. *Dakota Fanning*. Mitchell Lane Publishers, 2006.

McElroy, Lisa Tucker. *Love, Lizzie: Letters to a Military Mom*. Albert Whitman, 2005.

McMillan, Bruce. *Mouse Views: What the Class Pet Saw*. Holiday House, 1993.

Medina, Jane. *Tomas Rivera*. Harcourt, 2004.

Mendez, Phil. Black Snowman. Scholastic, 1989.

Micklos, Jr., John. *Grandparent Poems*. Wordsong/Boyds Mill Press, 2004.

Mora, Pat, and Charles Ramírez Berg. *The Gift of the Poinsettia = El regalo de la flor de nochebuena*. Piñata Books, 1995.

N

Nash, Margaret. The Best Snowman. Picture Window Books, 2003.

Nolan, Janet. *A Father's Day Thank You*. Albert Whitman, 2007.

O

Oppenheim, Joanne. *The Miracle of the First Poinsettia: A Mexican Christmas Story*. Barefoot Books, 2006.

P

Parish, Peggy. *Thank You, Amelia Bedelia*. HarperCollins, 1993.

Parker, Toni Trent. Snowflake Kisses and Gingerbread Smiles. Scholastic, 2002.

Polacco, Patricia. *Thank You, Mr. Falker*. Philomel Books, 1998.

Prevost, John F. *Evergreen Trees*. Abdo & Daughters, 1996.

Pulver, Robin. *Christmas for a Kitten*. Albert Whitman, 2003.

Purmell, Ann. *Christmas Tree Farming*. Holiday House, 2006.

R

Robertson, J. Jean. *Meet my Grandparents*. Rourke Publishing, 2007.

Rylant, Cynthia. Henry and Mudge and the Snowman Plan: The Nineteenth Book of Their Adventures. Simon & Schuster, 1999.

S

Schaefer, Lola M. *What's Up, What's Down?* Greenwillow Books, 2002.

Schertle, Alice. All You Need for a Snowman. Harcourt, 2002.

Sherman, Josepha. Flakes and Flurries: A Book About Snow. Picture Window Books, 2004.

St. George, Judith. *Make Your Mark, Franklin Roosevelt!* Philomel Books, 2007.

St. George, Judith. *Take the Lead, George Washington!* Philomel Books, 2005.

St. George, Judith. *You're on Your Way, Teddy Roosevelt!* Philomel Books, 2004.

St. Pierre, Stephanie. *What the Sea Saw*. Peachtree Publishers, 2006.

Sullivan, Sarah. *Dear Baby: Letters from Your Big Brother*. Candlewick Press, 2005.

T

Tagliaferro, Linda. *The Life Cycle of a Pine Tree*. Capstone Press, 2007.

Tate, Nikki. *Grandparents' Day*. Annick Press, 2004.

Teague, Mark. *Dear Mrs. Larue: Letters from Obedience School*. Scholastic, 2002.

Teague, Mark. *Detective LaRue: Letters from the Investigation*. Scholastic, 2004.

Tremblay, Helene. *Letters from Ritang: A Family in Kiribati*. Portage & Main Press, 1997.

V

Van Steenwyk, Elizabeth. *When Abraham Talked to the Trees*. Eerdmans, 2000.

W

Wells, Rosemary. *Bunny Mail*. Penguin, 2004.

Wilder, Laura Ingalls. *West from Home: Letters of Laura Ingalls Wilder, San Francisco, 1915*. HarperCollins, 1974.

Wilkie, Katharine E. *George Rogers Clark: Boy of the Northwest Frontier*. Patria Press, 2004.

Winters, Kay. *Abe Lincoln: The Boy Who Loved Books*. Simon & Schuster, 2003.

Woodruff, Elvira. *Dear Levi: Letters from the Overland Trail*. Knopf, 1994.